Living Ginger

Living Ginger

Mike Doyle

Ekstasis Editions

Library and Archives Canada Cataloguing in Publication

Doyle, Mike
	Living ginger / Mike Doyle.

Poems.
ISBN 1-894800-55-9

	I.†Title.

PS8557.O9L58 2004	C811'.54	C2004-904406-0

© 2004 Mike Doyle

Cover art: Miles Lowry

Published in 2004 by:
Ekstasis Editions Canada Ltd.	Ekstasis Editions
Box 8474, Main Postal Outlet	Box 571
Victoria, B.C. V8W 3S1	Banff, Alberta T0L 0C0

Living Ginger has been published with the assistance of grants from the Canada Council for the Arts and the British Columbia Arts Council administered by the Cultural Services Branch of British Columbia.

For my grandchildren

Genevieve, Charlie,

Mina and Guthrie,

and for Alice,

a contributor

NOTE

My title is a phrase of the painter Jack B.Yeats, who once said that he aims in his work for, 'the living ginger of life.' This seeking for 'felt life' is not the fashion. As Susan Sontag puts it in 'The Aesthetics of Silence': in 'the new myth' of art, art 'exists to be overthrown and connives at its own abolition.' In 'the old myth': art is 'consciousness seeking to know itself.' Strangely, perhaps, I don't see how that can ever be entirely superseded. Rather than such overthrowing, I find wisdom in Don Paterson's version of a Machado 'proverb':

Light your poem from two angles:
one for the straight reading,
one for the sidelong.

CONTENTS

Whiffling

INVENTORY

notes towards a poetics

No, not infantry, you drongo!
This is not that kind of operation.
Besides, again, you've got the wrong inflection.
All things considered, or considering,
you could call this taking stock.
There's a kind of order, but there are gaps.
Like in a grocery store at the end of a hard day.

It's the order of randomness, come about
by whatever happens inside who, where, when
and why, and what may be needed or conjured from
the word store. Happenstance, there's a word
that might fit the cases, nearly full or hovering
on empty. Not verses that scan without a ripple,
but wry and ginger, there's the tipple.

There isn't a plot or a hero, only occasions.
Okay, okay, so let's try a putative hero
(we could put on a mask, and dub her Tabitha,
but that would be conniving towards some kind of plot),
so why not call him Stanley Park, for example,
and think of him that way, tall and slim,
lots going on inside, some of it dark as
the woods, some bright as the beach,
though without a preconceived pattern, or rather
with a bustle of occurrences, furtive, funny,
rueful or ludicrous, to take a measure of.

A lottery of mood and circumstance,
that's another way of seeing it: improvisations
wrought from loves and deaths, language and memory,
ways the spirit has sorted, how it has talked to itself
from infantry to approaching senility.
If you seek a thread, it's woven among the lines.

25 February 2004

EL CUARTO BLANCO

for Lies Wiegman

I sleep
in a white room:
white walls
white ceiling
curtains white;
a Mexican overhead light
shaped like a soccer ball
pieced together from hexagons
of milkwhite glass;
rickety dresser
white metal shelves
shrouded in a white sheet.
I even have a white pisspot.

Then colour begins to seep in.
On the wall, above
pale bedsheets,
a large poster-photograph
in grey & white:
Paris street scene
cafe habitues
black coffee, white cups
waiter in a white jacket
two lovers leaning together
against a plane tree bole
under an offwhite sky.

Next to this on the chalkwhite
wall, another
white sky photograph:
junked cars piled high askew
three of them white-toned
in the unkempt grey grass;
foregrounded:

stalk-smothered white body
& large white head
of an abandoned doll
derelict child
open-eyed, landed akimbo
flung through a smashed car window.

Above my head
on the room's side white wall
a greywhite poster:
Recuerdos de Frida Kahlo –
sentimental, this Frida,
chocolate-box Virgin.

Now, scattered about my bed,
enters more colour:
bedframe, small tables, chairs,
a long carved bench
all in unpainted wood;
chiselled wood ikon
Virgin of Guadeloupe
robed in carmine & blue
standing
on the head of the crouching peasant
whose vision she was.
Her bodylength halo
goldpainted wooden spearheads,
a sturdy lustre.

She's surrounded by my few books:
baubles in a blue folder,
yellow *The Magic Mountain,*
the wise Montaigne green
& white. Also a black
Bible, from which I copy
in shaky calligraphy
The Song of Solomon.

Above the dresser
I've hoisted two orange bolsters
leaching all colour
from the lithographed Mayan head
nearby – acquiline nose,
anthracite eye, blackface,
yellow ochre headdress.

By a glass door across the room
a computer-age demon
squarehead black blockheater
cowers under the spread wings
of an angel, three-foot tall,
shaped from luminous silver
metal, holding towards me
a cup & saucer, receptacle
for a giant candle's
white glow.

White is our bridal colour.
Shall I mate with pale
romantic Frida
if she'd step down from her frame?
The Parisian lovers
are perhaps a hint,
but then there's the dead white doll.
Or would a room like this
suit only a *mariage blanc*?
White is their colour of death
from *los muertos* on out
but here I am, pink & alive
in bed on a Sunday morning
scribbling this nonsense
under a counterpane
of mustard yellow.
Glancing over my shoulder

I find carved on a bedpost
a keel-billed toucan
wooden testament
to a live, if clumsy, hand.

Time to get out of bed.
I swivel, place bare feet
white, on the chilly floor –
puce bricks, colour of flesh
inside the *cuerpo,*
or the last flush of nightfall
when, with a closing of blinds
I enter the white box of sleep.

For now the curtains are opened
the oyster dawn dispersed
the heavens clear blue.
Soon I shall step out into
the rival blue
of jacaranda, the sky
high up & far away
bleached white.

San Miguel de Allende,
February-March, 1999

ONE PLACE AT A TIME

San Miguel de Allende, 1999.
At unpredictable intervals
the cheap plastic chair
(courtesy the same soft drink
company whose empty bottle
Levi-Straus stumbled upon
deep in the Amazon
rainforest) shifts with a
jerk under my bum.
Am I riding a pig?

The faded sun umbrella
catches a drift of pepper tree
leaves, & twigs of bedraggled
jacaranda, in the small
paved *jardin* graced with a friend's
bas reliefs on the stone wall,
sculpted heads guarded by cacti.

Ubiquitous poinsettia,
bougainvillea, & among
statues halfhidden by the green
of basil, wild geranium,
calla lilies about to bloom,
spider plant, marigolds,
other plants who choose
to remain anonymous,
including one whose base mimics
a giant pineapple flourishing
spiky two-edged blades
curved like the underjaw
of a crocodile and, above these,

18

sharpbladed fans each poised
like a green monstrance, but bearded
as if the Host had shredded
into soft wispy threads, for
plucking by scarlet-breasted birds,
Mexican robins, to weave nests,
unaware of rapacious jaws
or green suns made of swords.

The span of hairs forms a fine net
beneath which dutifully dull
I at last read *The Magic Mountain.*
Prolix, over-explanatory,
scattered with humourless humour,
yet with concerns close to
my history, so I plod on, willing myself
through the morning's quota.

Then for a pep-up leaf idly
through Milosz poems, pausing
at "On the Road" (caught perhaps
by the Kerouac title?). Brief,
it's approximately dated:
St. Paul de Vence, 1967.

That year, driving a rental car,
heading north from Imperia,
along with that era's wife, still
conversible, & three sons
squirming in back.

"To what summoned?" Milosz poses
The urgent, imperious question as he
travels "through the blue myrrh
of dimmed churches" (so, not Matisse).
To what, indeed? I drove my family
far to the north towards a planned
English destination. So much
was certain, but I foresaw
nothing, feeling no need to see.

What I remember
many times in that French region–
baguette at noon, cheese, a bottle
of *vin ordinaire* by the roadside. Nor
yet had I claimed a heritage
much less had it snatched away.
That was a time of the senses.

Three decades on, canopied
by jacarandas, this, too,
albeit sadder and later,
a time of the senses,
but I don't need telling
what it must have been like,
that other man's journey
through the unattainable valley,
to his spot by the wailing wall.

2/99

20

WHIFFLING

for F. S.

'Will youse give us a whiff', they'd say,
not meaning the puff of a white Sunday,
but yerra a smoke, though sometimes
a draught or a shot of booze in the Crown
when they'd be 'passing dry', a whiff, a whiffle,
a sniff or inhalation, though in other places
at other times a whiffle's angling for mackerel
with a hand line from a swiftly
moving boat; but either way a whiffler
may be a trifler, an idle talker
out of both sides of a loose mouth
– do you get the drift?
                       A long while
back, wearing chain mail, armed
with javelins, body-axes,
swords, or staves, in early nineteenth-century
Norwich, for example, whifflers
formed a regular detachment
of the Corporation procession.
Three hundred years before that
'wyffelers on fote' carried
'slaugh swordes or javelynes'
'to kepe the peple in araye'. Yet

by 1660 whifflers were dismissed,
'contemptible fellows' (OED); whiffling:
- 'trifling, pettifogging, fussy',
'paltry, insignificant', and 'piffling'.

2.

'Moving lightly as if driven by gusts of wind' –
that's also whiffling. A couple of years ago,
at the National Gallery, Dublin,
picked up a print of Jack B.Yeats's
painting, 'This Grand Conversation
was under the rose': A woman
in full-length black seems to lean against
a blue and dun horse, while across a gap
to the right of the painting sits
a bowed figure 'white as a ghost'
or a man swathed in bandages,
stark against the greenery behind him.
Between and above woman and man,
highlighted against a dark tree bole,
a tiny pale pink rose. Separating the human
figures, a dusky sky over
the light-sourced green. The painting's
title alone hints symbolism, but
with Jack B it's the brushwork,
characterised by Sargent as a 'ruffling
like flags', similarly the scholar-poet-writer
Tom Paulin, taking the painter's hint
from his prose work *The Amaranthers,*
sums up: 'a ballad singer walking home
with a bundle of ballads "flittering in his hands".
This flittering or "whiffling" quality…essential to
the profound surface excitement of the paintings'.

And this is so. The poetry is in the paint.
The whole genius of this painter
stems from his impasto, the whiffling
character of his painting, just as,
comparably yet in contrast, the
fluid quality of Sebald's writing ('eddies')
consists of a flowing together, a subtle
whiffling of language, image, and memory.

11-13 February 2004

One Thing or Another

Speak to the things about you
                    - Jack Matthews

They speak for themselves. Why answer them
back? They may grow, or they may go,
or just go on. I don't know for how long
I've has this pebble on my windowsill.
Clothed now in a fine coating of dust,
it has had its own adventures, little
to do with me. I've simply lived along
beside it. Someone before me took it
in my view with a wrongheaded notion,
to the rockhound shop to have it polished.
It came to me, I've forgotten how,
as a natural stone, except for this sheen
which reflects the light from a hundred-watt
bulb in the ceiling. I'd just as soon have
found it on the beach, sea-washed or
sand-polished. In any case what can I tell it?
Somewhere in there, in that heart of stone,
it may have felt all these things, including
though seldom, the caress of my warm hand
as I've pick it up for a moment, absently.
Why would it want to know about me?

PEBBLE ON WINDOWSILL

Put there, God knows when, but probably
absentmindedly, on a windy day after
walking the beach, anywhere from Shoal Bay
to Island View, but here it is, ready to be kicked
if only Dr Johnson could fight his way out
from the pages of Boswell's *London Journal* across
the room. Then maybe it's from a warped perspective
only that this stone is inside this room on this
windowsill? Perhaps it gazes out with longing
at the other pebbles on the garden path which lead
to the compost's succulence, the possibility
of recycling, by gradual stages, into a rich loam?

Or maybe that gets it all wrong, and this room
like a sort of architectural Alice-in-Wonderland
but less sure of itself longs to be telescoped
so it can curl up in foetal position
inside this stone never needing to look out?
Meantime, fixed here, inside the room created
somehow out of random thoughts, undisciplined,
or imagination, yearning, to seal itself
inside a cell of security inside an airy
dwelling dreaming of ultimate reduction,
to be oval and smooth and speckled akin to this pebble
which one shift of thought can render
into the shell of a new life, one circle nearer.

Rapacities

the rapacity of eros - John Updike

WRITTEN ON THE SOUL

H.M.D. 1928-1958

A July winter among the drab Scots stone,
rain squalls, southerly buster; icy nodes
scour my face. But you feel nothing.
I look down at your stillness, your last smile,
but your eyes are closed. You do not see me.

Our long ago shared life, short, not nasty,
at least in itself, the nights of closeness, when
you were home, days of gentle companionship.
Quiet friends, for a while, in our small life.
Now your eyes are closed. You do not see me.

Everything gone. You were already far
away when it finally ended. Once you said,
'It's slow suffocation, Mikey', speaking
more than you knew, for both of us.
Now your eyes are closed. You do not see me.

And now, distant in time and place, it grieves me
yet again that our days and nights are done:
sunset at Waikaremoana, the fruit harvest
in South Otago. They go on. I go on,
but your eyes are closed. You do not see me.

An unseen finger and thumb closed your eyelids,
as I had closed mine to you before it was done.
Yet I can see your smile on our garden slope
still in my soul, grieve on, have words to speak,
but your heart is closed. You will not hear them.

Dear love, for so you were, where now
the sheen of your hair, our quiet being together,
your young hands clasping my shoulders,
your humour and courage? I cannot find them.
I am here still, seeing you. You do not see me.

THE YELLOW ROOM

Wadestown, 1953

Perching on an eroded hillslope
our flat faced down the windswept valley.
Bedroom, livingroom, kitchen, bath,
its living space a yellow room:
brown haircord, Danish furniture,
a Roland Hipkins watercolour
over the mantlepiece, Lake Taupo
behind a march of sunny poplars;
pencil drawing of a wood stove
by old McCormick; I have it
still to waken to each morning
alongside a photo of my mother
1920s style, the stove
familiar from my 1930s schoolroom.

I have none of your shoreline sketches.
From you I have a King James Bible,
on India paper, pocket-sized,
the two-volume Chambers Shakespeare
I've rarely used in fifty years,
but where the print of a Miro hessian
or Picasso's ink Don Quixote
vanished to I have never known.
These were the things we owned together.
Two young lovers in our twenties,
content among them. You slowly died.
We slowly lost our innocence.
When you were gone, I abandoned them.
But nothing of it has ever left me.

24 January 2004

MEMENTO

for Nettie Anderson

Scored in the heavy bark
two pair initials,
surrounded by a heart
pierced by an arrow.

a lifetime later,
the carver discovers
her own initials, deeply
embedded; cannot remember

who the other pair stood for.
On the blunted arrow tip
a small trickle of sap
poises, like dried blood.

12.99

AT THE DUTCH BAKERY

early 1980s

I always see you
one bright cold day
in early spring, maybe,
crossing Fort Street,

jaunty smile
in a slim fur coat
maroon corduroy cap.
The jauntiness

because you were late,
better than twenty minutes,
no excuses – just
impudent bravado.

Yet again I was angry,
hot with it, on the sidewalk,
though nipped by frost.
But not so cold

as now in the white heat
of your rage, in a time
when you're always on time,
but never there. I'd like

just once more, to meet
who you were then,
not to turn back the clock,
but to see if we'd still warm

each other. You'd never wear
a fur coat now, but instead
would carry a banner protesting
seal hunts, leghold traps, the yoke

of conjugality.
Where has she gone, who you were?
How I'd love to find her!
Yes, I know it can't happen

again. But I loved you then,
in fury & perplexity,
frustration, tenderness.
Could I love you now?

In spite of a spate of
words, words, words,
there's a depth of anguish
I'll never be able to speak for.

Why did that impudent image,
coat, cap, fine oval head,
lodge its barbed tip in me?
I don't know. Once, it hurt

wonderfully, in there, deep,
that's all I know.
But, now I have 'leisure for fiction',
can I write it off?

CORRESPONDENCE

How many more times
will I write you a note
and not send it? Today,
this morning in a quiet
house, not ours, mine,
clearing my desk, I find
the latest such scribble,
a plea, always, but what
am I asking, hoping for?

Once, I returned
every photo of you I had:
from you at nineteen,
lissom, lithe, small-breasted,
profile like Nefertiti,
to you at fifty,
face-on to the camera,
a look caught between
insouciance, insolence.

That first photo
followed by passion, commitment.
children, a life together,
then the erosions – slow
at first, and invisible,
but gathering momentum
to end in a landslide,
– a mere metaphor, telling
nothing, yet telling all.

And the second?
One of a pair, the other
missing, mine. Both mask
convenient lies, unspeakable
blames, and a rage – or two
one a firestorm, the other
a slow burn
still smouldering, between
the notes, which add to the smoke.

OTHERNESS

It's you! Stamping your foot
at the edge of the sea
near Karekare, some place
other than here, some time
other than now. And you.

If only, here and now,
I could listen to your angry
denials, denunciations
seeing their contradiction
in all your body language.

Merely and simply me,
I'm here where you are not,
I'm now when you were then,
wishing your salted words
could sting my ears once again

or better your lips on mine
tasting of sea-salt, you
a dripping mermaid
at, let's say, Opononi,
or was it some other place
some other time? Wherever
it was I want us there
and want the sand
and waves washing the sand
at that time and that place
seeping between my toes
for landfall, as I bend
my lips to yours,
at one time all the otherness
I wanted, but here and now
melted down into words.

TOUJOURS PARIS

mid 1980s

At the Cafe des Poetes
Avenue des Gobelins
the coffee's great.

She thaws morning hands
on a bowl of cafe au lait
while, with the back of a spoon,

he crushes two sugar cubes
each into two nips of
espresso, mopping up

dregs with a third.
Thus warmed and sweetened they
stroll back to the Hotel de Dada.

On their way through the plane trees,
sharpened by frosty air
their words become kitchen knives

jabbing and piercing repeatedly.
They fret behind the long windows;
the drying garments

scattered at random
on radiator and shower-rail,
ignored flags of truce.

HUMMINGBIRDS

Three inch snowfall on the deck;
half empty hummingbird feeder
frozen to the waist.
                              Beneath
the duvet, floating towards siesta
you drift back to last summer's haziness:
footsteps across the duckboards,
light knock at the French windows:
there she was, as if a neighbour,
accustomed to calling in
most days, come now, at last, in search
of a cup of tea. You sat at the kitchen table
facing each other, the round surface
no ouija board, simply a flat plane:
milk jug, plate of digestives,
cups and saucers, red paper IKEA
napkins, left over from Christmas.

'It seems so natural', she said,
as if you had no quarrel, then or ever,
nor gone divergent unfamiliar ways.
For a moment you sat in an empty room
stripped bare of family pictures,
only the oblongs darker on the walls
where those mementoes had hung so comfortably.

But as you tilted the pot to pour the tea
in the small cloud of steam
a new picture began to form.
After she'd gone, the silence would leave you questions:
how to mount it and frame it, what to see in it,
in what space of your life it should be kept.

The hummingbird feeder, half full
that summer afternoon,
could be replenished any time.

3 January 2004

CROSSED WIRES

(message snagged by
my answering machine)

He: Hello!

She (flat):   Yes.

He: Hello.

She (still flat): Hi.

He: Who's this?

She: You called our house, Bill.

He (resentfully): I did not!

MY PLACE, OR YOURS?

The mind in its own place - JM

'Okay, I'll come on up,
but can't stop long.'

Hey, here's one weird suburb,
a trepidation,
maybe a joy at that?
A risk, at any rate.
You note the hovering
lowrises, bland but secretive
facades in fading sunlight,
everything seems to quiver
on a dark edge. Farther along,
a church's grey brick frontage
opposite law courts, grey.
All oddly speculative.

You follow her, passing
a market: whitecaparisoned
servitors portioning
blocks of a lardy substance
with wires, alongside pyramids
of fleshy fruit, nectarines,
peaches, plums,
a tumble of bananas,
banality, the normal,
formally reassuring.

If it's like that up there
no worries, but it all
depends on her, while seeming
to be an affair of you both.

Looking into a cafe window
you see a girl slumped over
a miserable cup. The girl
you're with perhaps, some other
time, not knowing you?
You follow on, soon come
to a door. She has the key.

An entry to warmth and closeness?
A tiny mechanism
holding you to a future
unforeseen, arriving
with a quick quarter turn
of one slender wrist?

YSSA

(i)

She was there all right: in a body
oh such a body, and eyes
…and what more need be,
enough to catch your attention.
You saw her from time to time
at first, then inescapably.

She moved into you, slowly
but surely, she moved into you.
That done she began
to metamorphose. This ordinary
woman whose eyes had lost
something of life, whose mind
looked out towards limited
horizons, once housed in you
seemed to be someone new. Her
eyes gained light and beauty,
her body, already beautiful
in its unawareness, became
an enchantment to the soul,
her mind a meeting place.

(ii)

Like a fade-out scene in a movie:
framed by a house on the shore
a small figure raised by steps,
posed rigid as a toy soldier,
key poised at the doorlock, then seen
no more. But there had been other
times: cross-legged on a sofa,
lotus posed, or curled

into you like a child,
an impulse, another pose,
acting in some private play?
And once, excusing a cruel
act, sat by your side
covertly pushing a hip
against yours - in sudden warmth,
a complicit message,
obfuscation?

Then, rewinding the reel
to a time of new acquaintance,
an early day in a cafe:
seeing you, she strode over
to kiss you full on the lips.

Then, betweentimes, indifference,
or so it seemed. Yet this small
pantheon of gestures
planted her in your soul
as if she had no place to go
yet wished to be there with you
on her own terms only,
private and gamesome,
in a game with hermetic rules.
Or no game at all?

(iii)

You saw her out there still
kept her inside illumined,
continued to gaze at her,
but could go no further.
There was no meeting, no
transformation. You
held, but could not know her.

It was as if you had given
shelter to a lost soul,
but could never reach her,
Sometimes at night as if
you'd lost your own soul

in a dream. Still searching for her,
trying to realise the
enchantment of absorption,
slowly you were losing…
Where are you? Who is in
whose dream? How and when
was it conjured? You
were there all right to begin with.
Where does she come in?

NIGHT WANDERINGS

Home late from the party, too much on my mind,
sleeping fitfully, waken in the night,
glimpse an old moon through a chink in the curtain;
up to wander among sleepers, ghosts of my past

selves, I remember you, here, not so long ago,
lying next to the current of these selves, hangdog,
downturned crescent of lips thinly mocking the moon,
as you lay there, tensed and unwilling, on the bed's far edge.

You have disappeared, but I wander restlessly
from room to room. Is it you I seek
or one of the ancient ghosts, to commiserate,
as we search vainly in the deepening spaces?

Drawing the curtains open, I look out upon
wan shifty shadows of shrubs on monochrome lawn.
Are you lingering there among them, or have you
escaped already over the ramshackle fence?

If you are still out there, shall I beckon you home?
If you are gone shall I learn at last it meant
this is the way it would go from the beginning?
Looking askance, I see one of my younger selves

holding aside the other end of the curtain,
in an attitude the mirror image of mine.
Like me, he has searched within and now, like me,
looks outward, seeking you, but seeing nothing.

AT THE POST OFFICE

The last of January: needling rain.
Cold in the streets, subdued bustle:
bodies parcelled up against the weather.
To the bank, hardware seeking batteries,
post office for stamps, all forward-looking
activities. Last evening she had come
back; you cooked her a dinner; she
stayed four hours, seeming reluctant
to leave, to resume their living apart,
this modern solution to the angst
of alienation, disguised
as a need for solitude, though nothing
akin to Wordsworth's bliss, or anyone's.

At the post office, the new packets of stamps
had shrunk. You said: 'They look slimmer!'
(The way you feel, yourself, these singular days).
The girl, the sturdy one, said: 'Here,
let me check, to see that they're all there.'
And you: 'That's what I have to do every morning,
when I wake up!' The other girl, the slim one,
laughed so much she blossomed before your eyes.
For a brief spell, a whole world warm and fulsome.

30 January 2002

ON THE ROAD,
WAKING SLOWLY

A wall
            a dresser
the empty
            half of a bed
closed curtains
            a silence
transfixing
            intervals
a tap's loud drip
            on metal
a clock tick
            marking
time unseen
            the dark
just perceptibly
            changing
shapes until
            you, yourself
subtly gradated
            blacks then greys
then hodgepodge
            find
a shape, the room
            the window
buildings beyond
            the streets
at last you could give
            this place
a name
            in turn

it can tell you

        who you are

but never

        why

August 2001

TOUCH AND GO

reading Stanley Kunitz's 'Touch Me'

A gazebo in Valentine's Park:
her words, a stab to the heart,
last of the first time. He
crazed with love, torn apart,
turned aside, and wept.
Then the familiar pain
the wild joy come again
a dozen years later
now forty-odd years ago
this time for a longer visit,
the wildness wilder yet
but it came out the same in the end
eight thousand miles from where
it had begun. Not in a park
this time, by a breakwater,
her words a stab to the heart.

He was not done with it yet.
Though twenty years went by
the arrow sought him out
missing her by the thickness
of a skin. They fell to without
falling, together, in love.
Came a day when she'd done
with whatever it was for her.
Arriving at the seismic door
his knock met only silence.

Three gifts for his gift of desire.
For the first he was too young.
The second took up his life,
or most of it, ending in bitter
words. The third had come,
unbidden interruption.
Through it he discovered
no one to answer to
only himself. Belatedly
these words, neither stab nor silence,
words, at the end of desire.

BEN TROVATO

remembering Trezh

(i)

Midsummer; yet the mind of winter, holding
'nothing that is not there and the nothing that is';
then, like a footnote, Simic in the *New Yorker*
a few years back, confessing he 'failed miserably
at imagining nothing'. Doesn't surprise me, but then
it depends on what you mean. Tristan Tzara,
for one, an adept at imagining nothing
concrete, scribbled nonsense poems, sounds
merely. But can *merely* be nothing? It depends,
like a wheelbarrow and white chickens in the rain.
'Something always came to keep me company',
says Simic. Lucky fellow! Would I could conjure up
Trezh from sixty years ago, choppy blonde
hair snuggling into my chest, beestung lips,
like cuddling a teddy bear. You can imagine
the rest and so, alas, can I. Nothing to it!

(ii)

Never again that riverbank with its thin
gratuitous stretch of sand, never again
you, or someone like you, touching a bow
to omnivorous lips, or opening them
into a quiver of flowers, me poised above it
a bee eager for honey. In a far country
long ago, but maybe you live and are well?
So be it. You were a joy to me, all physical,
nothing that needed thought. But for now all I can do
is think of you. I see sand, wet rock, logs leaning
together shaping a tepee, tyre tracks tamped in the wet,
a dog with a stick returning to its master;
but this sand sifts by an ocean. You are not here,
nor anyone like you. Nor anyone like I was,
stunned by summer, packed with latent energy,
all wished upon you.

                    Now, I wish for nothing,
hearing the traffic surge past on a gritty road
to nowhere in particular. I look at a tiny
crab in a shallow pool and see myself,
scuttering hither and yon, with no mind, a mereness.
Somehow I've conjured you up, a longing, also
a thanks for eyes the colour of this sea,
lips that were open, open, open.

August 5-14, 2002

Insouciance

NIGHT

The blinds won't stop their clatter.
Out there
Arctic blasts
bruise the dark.

Warmer here in bed
but what scenario
to lull me? You got it, Marilyn! –
Some Like It Hot.

Warm breezes from below
billow up her skirt.
She tries to hold it down
oh so fetchingly!

But here's Willem Dafoe
eye cocked on her.
His fingernails have grown
another inch.

It's 4 AM.

THE CROSSING

Szymborska's
'Elegiac Calculation'

On reading
the translation
in daily search
for 'inspiration'
ransacked
seeking a 'trigger'
so let's get going
before rigor
sets in: *nota*
a friend died
due on the rota
this was Hemi
in November
then still a man
then briefly embers
so I'm told
who unlike me
did not cross
the well lit threshhold
of last Christmas
but passed away
that's what they say
to soften it
up here up yonder
down there Down Under
a threshhold I'll
not cross again.

As for the questions
if and differences

miffs and stiffs
we go alone
to where we go
whether we meet
someone we know
I'll cross that bridge
whenever I go
unless its another
bridge of Avignon
one end only
leading to none.

But now beginning
to play the game
no one but me
to take the blame
unless and if
you go there, so
we'll say goodbye
and then hallo.
If we meet with Hemi
he can play with you
while I write this,
Szymborska, too.
If not for her
what should I do?
(Today at least,
as sometimes, words
are not a feast).
Tomorrow, maybe,
next time, soon,
shall I play a
different tune?

5-6 January 2004

SOMETIMES YOU AIN'T GONNA MAKE IT

You can sit there
all you like
nothing will come
the page stark white.

Her eyes are lost
in trashcan lids;
Lear tries a howl
but burps and belches.

When you invite her
to come on up
see you some time
up comes the Doppel

so you stay home
to sit and brood
locked up inside
cold as a cod.

You cannot hack it
so go out
the movies maybe
Sean Penn pouts

curls his lip
fixes his gaze
you just sat there
in a daze.

But comes the time
you must unfreeze
pen alert
as you stroke her knees

6 January, 4 February 2004

Sitting Quietly
Doing Nothing
Spring Comes
And the Grass Grows
By Itself

*- Coach House Press
postcard, early1970s*

Mid-February
what shall I do
grass as thick
as a bear's pelt
in midwinter
ground too soft
to be mowed without
digging waterlogged
trenches. Mental
hibernation has me
Buridan's donkey
dithering which way
to turn. If only
the gardener
Arlene had not
quit to have kids
do her MA.
Jan, good to talk with
pretty besides
green-fingered
hardworking
elegant
doesn't cut grass.

Does she smoke, I wonder?

19 February 2004

NELLY'S FAREWELL

A back gate faded beige,
Brit 1930s style:
abundances of mock orange
welcome you to the garden.

Before you enter the gate,
near totes and potting soil
a rich carmine weigela
blossoms all spring.

Through and above it
climbing towards the eaves
on fishnet
a Nelly Moser clematis,
flowers a vaunting six inches
across, in subtle
gradations of mauvy pink.

Come summer
weigela flowers fade
deserting the pleasure
of their leaves' particular green.

Flamboyant Nelly blooms
wither to thin
brown parchments.

At the centre of each
one inch across
like tiny balls of thread
seedboxes spun in old gold
still cling to the net,
strange forms of sea anemone
out to enrapture the sun.

CHRISTMAS TO-DO

for Kegan

I bought a gift, especially for you.
Can't find it anywhere. What shall I do?
The whole thing has me feelin' kinda blue.

I've taken the house apart, every bolt and screw,
For several hours I've turned my life askew.
Frustration! Yes, I'm somewhat in a stew.

You're quite entitled to bawl me out and boo.
Searched everywhere from Ur to Timbuctoo,
But I'm afraid I just don't have a clue

Where else to look, though in two days I'm due
To load you with this gift. It must have flew
The loony coop, become the residue

Of ghosts, a revenant. I could get a new
Gift and give that to you. So please don't sue!
This billet doux, or considered apercu

Stands in for the replacement you'll accrue
If I find the first gift you can have that, too.
To clap my hands on it would be quite a coup.

Imagine the fanfarinade, the folfaroo!
I'll play a merry tune on my kazoo
Or purchase some fresh bibelot in lieu

Or sally forth to hire me a gumshoe.
Before the owl pips out 'Toowit! Toowoo!'
I'll have you something, or send me to the zoo

Where I'll have time to sit and brood, and rue
The giftless day, my witless cud to chew
While listening to the cows intone, 'Moo-ooo!'

But should I find it, then we'll have a brew,
A noggin for each member of the crew –
But careful! Don't imbibe that pot of glue!

Your physog will take on a sickly hue
At which perhaps your gift will turn ecru,
Both of you having said your, 'Tooraloo!'

Alas, I'm short of rhymes to make it new
unless I mention things that are taboo
or hints on how to boost up the tofu.

I haven't told the story of Brian Boru
or summarised *The Taming of the Shrew*
or made allusions to the manitou.

But here we are, alive and well, we two,
The giver and the givee, and it's pru-
Dential to solve the problem and work through

these difficulties to reach the best conclu-
sion for us both. I've searches to pursue!
One way or t'other, time to say, 'Adieu!'

Christmas 2001.

ABLUTIONS

A clearing cough,
a clink and a clank:
A toothbrush taking
its turn to leave
the beaker. The soap
solitary in its dish
waits for one hand.
A locked door
conceals the chinking
of glass, the taptaptap
of soapchoked razor
on porcelain bowl.
Q-tip, styptic pencil,
aftershave sting,
here where we're most
freely ourselves.

Hiss, drill of the shower
cloud of unknowing,
chafe of towel
on unseen back.
A flushing, flip
of a switch, a buzzing.
Mist clears from the
mirror, a face
recovers itself,
checks one more time
for nicks, missed patches.
A hand holding
a brush persuades
hair into place.
Click. The door opens.
A figure emerges
pushed out on a
small cloud of steam.

THE ROSE TATTOO

February 1948

for Richard Drury

Gone ashore, solo run,
pusser in doeskin fore-and-aft
short weekend leave
from barrack dorm in Chatham
slated for demolition
in Boney's time, a hundred
forty years earlier,
still standing more or less,
flat roof roughly turfed over;
once, splicing the mainbrace,
you'd snored off up there
in full summer afternoon sun
several hours, spent weeks
stripping sunburnt skin
from raw torso, writhing
in coarse hammock, unable
to report to Sick Bay, fearing
Defaulters.
                    Winter
before, one spell of three
weeks or so, several times
at Lights Out, bordering sleep
lay there watching your body
float ten feet in the air
under the nissenlike curve
of barrackroom ceiling.

Now
back to earth, gone ashore
to Dickens' Rochester
cringingly proud in that nineteen-
year-old body, found your
way to the tattoo parlour,

little chap in a khaki
overall, his hollow
needles, his rag, his bottle of
Dettol disinfectant
and mickey of Scotch, who sketched,
fine in blue outline – branch,
leaves, rose, swallow with flightwide
wings; filled in the colours:
red, green, blue, a rich brown,
bringing blood to the forearm's
surface, alternately
swabbing the wound with Dettol
swigging Scotch to steady his hand
never once applying
the wrong identical bottle.
So, Yorkists in retreat,
youth floated out of that parlour
a matelot, old salt, admiral
of your own imagination.

The ships would come later.

July 2001.

AT THE SPHINX'S FOOT

What more do you want?
All these years you've fixed me
with the same blank stare.

Whatever I do to please you
only in anger does your
expression seem to change.

No wonder I'm wary.
Your look pierces to the heart
of my confusion, yet

you remain implacable.
I'm here as in a waiting-room,
but what am I waiting for?

Is it your smile? But wouldn't
a smile like yours be a piercing
arrow, enigma, irony

at best? To please you
I cut off my living root; my
fantasies of fair women

stayed in the head. I carried
news of you everywhere,
but to me your fame is no joy.

I wrote you a thousand pages;
there's no sign you ever read
one. I can write no more.

Behind you the sun illumines;
I'm exposed to its fierceness,
parching for lack of shelter.

It scorches, & there's nowhere
to hide, except in the shade
at your feet. But there it's black

as the grave. At this late hour
I find I'm not quite ready
for that. I must make a move

if I can. I must go. But where?
How do I seek directions?
I'm going. But wait! Let me ask you…

WHAT SAY

If you know what you say
you know what you say you
know what you say you know.

If you say what you know
you say what you know you
say what you know you say

If what you say you know
what you say you know what
you say you know what you

If say you know what you
say you know what you say
you know what you say if

what you know you say if
what you know you say what
you know you say what you

If you if what if say
know what know you know if
say you say if say what

You know you say what you
say you know if what say
you say what if you know

you know what you say you
say if you say what you know
what you say you know if

know you say what you know
say you know what you say
if you say what you know.

LIVING GINGER

for Colm and Sally Brennan

When you told him what
you intended to title the book,
prideful on his pennyfarthing
teetering on a tightrope
stretched across a ravine,
mashie niblick in one hand,
tray of cocktails poised
in the other, he had 'the bit
between his teeth'. A conjuror
by mouth as well as manual
and pedal, he snorted: 'Musha,
why wouldyez want to call it
such a t'ing? Sure, what you intend is,
'Living gingerly!' Preening himself
swaying a time or two,
he almost swallowed the bit,
while muzzling up yet another
round of applause.

'True enough for ya', you told him.
'All I do is write'.

28 February - 2 March 2004

74

Lingering

A Contribution

We had the problem of age, the problem of wishing to linger.
Not needing, anymore, even to make a contribution.
                              - Louise Gluck, 'Arboretum'

for Peter Stevens

Assuredly, speaking for myself, I like this lingering
though believing death part of the parcel.
Whether you wish or not, if you are alive
to the world and have some gift of articulacy,
the 'contributions' come, come what may.
Whatever else comes triggers them. It's good
for example, to look at the finches, clustering
around the suet net hung in the garden, desired by
their kind, or to sit comfortably,
nine of us, family, mostly 'unwithered' young,
in the breakfastroom of the Sylvia Hotel
looking out to sea, red and black freighters
moored at intervals in the wintry bay,
and hearing a seagull's squawk, like a ringing telephone,
note that the next one doesn't sound anything like.

As to looking 'with no real avidity', well, yes,
almost a term for the birds. No, I'm not avid
any more, the real and unreal kinds both
seem to have escaped me, but this being alive
is, for the present, a likeable kind of thing.

Like any Horatian, I don't desire much:
to read, to write, to walk, watch movies, listen
to several kinds of music, and in the benevolent
season hack at a tennis ball. Winter's a time
for more Tai Chi, more *chi.* Go to the library
once in a while, but not to sit on your benches
or feed those pigeons. I don't even need to
search for new ways of writing poems,
new measures, new symbols, more aggressive images.
This lot will do. Deliberate disguises,
a thing of my past. Who'll publish? I don't care
much. All right, then, desire is inescapable,
though far from being 'a god'. If the young
are, as you say, offended by all this,
it's something I don't know about. But I am
curious. Why the hell should they be? They've
got it all coming, well, most of it, most of them.
I had a friend one time who couldn't stop working,
couldn't stop telling everyone: 'It's time
to *stop* and smell the roses!' A candidate
for your arboretum? Speaking of stopping,
it's time for me to quit, but only this poem.
When the lingering's over, that will take care of itself.

17 January 2000

EVA, MAISIE, AND NORA

for Margaret, then

Seeing them still, in the mind's eye,
these last three lodgers at Aunt Margaret's,
a clutch of sisters come to Cricklewood
from the bogs of Tipperary. Summer sun,
young women in their twenties, Eva the prettiest,
Maisie the likeable one, and Nora
always a little apart, this time smoking,
sat on the coping stone above the low brick wall,
while Eva and Maisie play a makeshift game
of King, on the street, its tarmac surface
squidgy, swamping the gravel. They
play with two little boys, my brother
and me, teasing us, throwing the tennis ball
just out of reach, Eva in high good humour,
cheeks ruddy with effort, eyes asparkle,
laughing as we dive to catch the ball
missing by a whisker. Then Nora begins
a song, not Irish this time, languorous:
'When the deep purple falls…'

At length we are called inside, slipping
on loose squares of linoleum. The dark
has come again. Soon Bill and I
wriggle under hot sheets, but first we have
a grace, the moment when Aunt Margaret opens
her bottle of red biddy; as she carelessly
closes the front room curtain we catch a glimpse
of Uncle Steve, not too drunk this time, taking
off his bicycle clips and as he bends to it
letting a huge fart, at which Maisie laughs aloud
a sound of raunchy mischief.

Now Margaret has the squeezebox and a cigarette,
glass of biddy alongside, begins to play -
'Rody McCorley', 'The Rising of the Moon'.
Later, from the hot bedroom above,
we'll hear the girls, voices slower and slower
as the wine slows Margaret's hands, now it's
'Lament for the Irish Emigrant', 'Let Erin Remember',
and the waited-for finale, 'Danny Boy',
then silence. I see them down there, drinking
tea by now, with Margaret's homemade poundcake.
As I drift into sleep I know they'll be reading
the tealeaves, portentous about a future.

This was in 1940. Within weeks
Margaret and Steve, talking 'invasion', scurried
back to Ireland. I would meet them again
only once, briefly, in their dark cottage
in Borrisokane, its walls three feet thick.
I never again saw Eva, Maisie, and Nora,
nor heard a thing about them, but can see them
any time, back through sixty-odd years,
young girls in their twenties, on short commons,
aglow in the pathos of a treacherous hope.

February 2002

TOWARDS HELENSVILLE

Early 1960s: For J.B.

Half a world away
half a lifetime ago
sleeping under the stars
under pohutukawa:
two sleeping bags, tarpaulins
to ward off heavy dew,
shorthaul, not even a campfire.

Tuckered out
after a day's tramping
towards the mountains,
a whiff of hotsprings
a long way from our bourgeois
selves. A closeness of friends.

Otherwise, why would I be
there, not home in bed
in a warm room
my partner spooned in my lap
asleep, after the only thing.

But that was then. Thanks
for your Christmas e-mail. I'll
answer soon, with an inventory
of my own infirmities,
my count, not of sperm
but of liver spots,
far enough from home.

1 January 2004

LEAVING BORRISOKANE

for Bill, shared memories

You were going on nine, Billy
just seven, coming home
to his birthplace. Late 1930s:
Holyhead to Dun Laoghaire
overnight mailboat, grungy
upper deck scattered with lounging
Micks quietly snuffling
together, awkwardly splayed
against bulkheads, groping for
hard corners to snooze in
fitfully until dawn. Train from Dublin,
finally at Clockjordan
in pelting rain, overhearing
the 'latest news': some poor sod
had taken a potshot
at the Prince of Wales. A taxi
at the garage, open sides
under a canvas top flittering
in the breeze. The mechanic,
nodding at the driver's back,
told us, "Yiz'll need to watch
that fella, one a them protestants.'

Later, 'at home' in Borr',
out in the donkey-and-cart with
your taciturn Granda, Bill
Carroll, trudging the peatbog,
watching him bent double
cutting peat, yourself edging
timidly not too close

to the lip of waterlogged
pits; Grandma Norah scattering
scant fistfuls of grain to scrawny
chickens; you running up the yard
tripping over cheapsandalled
heels onto a random
nettlebed, or strolling
to the shebeenlike corner
store, a gossoon hovering
over you, thrusting
from his one good hand a
penny bar of Nestle's chocolate,
saying, in admonition: "Now
be sure and tell your Mammy
'twas Pat Molloy that's after
giving you this!' Arrah, musha,
they'd say, a class of thing you
couldn't give voice to, your mother
dead and gone these two years past,
last seen as a wraith
in back of a London taxicab.

You remember the big black tarpaulin
tent and thumbstruck projectionist
when one pale summer evening
'strange' Aunt Chrissie treated us
to Fredric March's new movie,
Les Miserables. The first attempt

at a showing, the reel of film
wound upside down, or back to front,
everyone in the village sloping in free
next evening. Your aunt, stiff tears
glistening in sapphire eyes
under a thatch of natural carroty hair,
stood to rigid attention
as the gramophone, wound
just-as-tight, thumped out:
'Soldiers are we, who fought
and died for Ireland,
against the foe from a...'

          Then
at last in the train once more,
slatted wood seats heavily varnished,
yiz both heaving and pulling
wood bodywork, energetic
to bully the chuffering old
engine to bursting point,
the sooner to reach Dun Laoghaire.
return to the 'land across the sea,'
the recollected joy
of a copy of Mickey Mouse.

Little you knew then, either of you,
that the pull 'ever afterwards'
would be to go back, go back,
but it would not get you there.

June-July 2004

NOVEMBER DAY,
PACIFIC COAST

for Douglas Craik, and
his Sibelius 78s

Early morning sky
duck egg blue with a scarf
of luminous pink,
the framing of my neighbour's
unfinished kayak shed
orange against dank green
grass and above it
swaying on an offshore wind
grey branches and twigs
of birch trees sporting
a few barely surviving
flags of tattered yellow.

A workday silence
out there, an untested
silence in here
proves placid as morning
continues on.
Blue porcelain birdbath
surfaced with ice,
birdfeeder waiting
for me to get up and fill it,
while frost has killed
the hanging basket of fuchsias.

For an instamatic moment,
at the hummingbird feeder's
scarlet horn and yellow grid
a solo flyer
wittering fluttering darting

in his strange coat
of iridescent khaki
conjures up sixty odd
years ago, early in a war
seen through a tiny window
a city somewhere in Europe
antiblast crisscrosses
of sticky paper and icicles
dripping from eavestroughs,
a khaki clad
soldier kicking ice
from the gutter
going at it in fits and starts
stopping from time to time
to blow on red fingertips
sticking like claws
through khaki mitts his breathing
a vapour trail
through khaki balaclava,
five years of war up ahead.

November 2003

AFTER THE SNOWMELT

remembering Inge

Walking north towards the village
top of Oliver Street,
last block an inviting downhill
curve, happened upon

a brand new pair of skis,
stood in the crook of a gnarled
stunted crouching old tree,
poised at the ready

on the rough grey shoulder,
sheep'swool sweater,
of a grimly vigilant troll
dug in for the next heavy swirl.

8, 15 January 2004

RAKING SHAKING

for Gwladys Downes

Set to talk about poetry
looking for Navajo
chants of propitiation
hauled out Jerry Rothenberg's
Shaking the Pumpkin
shook out a couple of pages
stripped thirty years ago
from *Greenfield Review*
poems by Harold Littlebird
N. Scott Momaday, &c,
one with an epigraph
famous words from Hokusai:
'at ninety I shall have penetrated
to the essence of all things…'

Wonderful! I need
to propitiate something
every day in myself
to move a little nearer
that same essence.
Seventy-four now, fortunate
in the blessed privacy
of an all too occasional
calling, somehow
once in a while a
true poem finds me.

This just to note it.
A note of thanks
before I go out
raking November leaves.
But that's what I'm doing
in here, already,
raking November leaves
for a glimpse of the pure

yellows, the burnished reds,
rapt in their beauty,
wrapped in the rhythm
of arm, elbow, and rake,
enraptured by the certainty
of a greenness to come,
and the cycle of yellow,
brown, red, and the green
to come, the green
that will keep on coming.

November 2002

GETTING ALONG

to Alice

Late February, pink
suffuses the clouds
as pale blue sky
leaches gradually

to pearl. This happens
around us, without
agency. You
glance up from the

stove, remarking:
'Blossom is out
all up and down
the boulevard'.

This the outside
of what you see.
I turn from a thought
find what you've said

in the mind's eye
by now, the pink
evaporated,
sky clear blossom.

'It'll keep on coming',
I say, not knowing exactly
what that might mean.
'That's the good of it',

you say; I know
what you mean. In
the space between us,
you the conduit:

That we are here.
That we can look.
That we can speak of it
to each other.

22 February 2003